How to Draw the Life and Times of
Chester A. Arthur

Rachel Damon Criscione

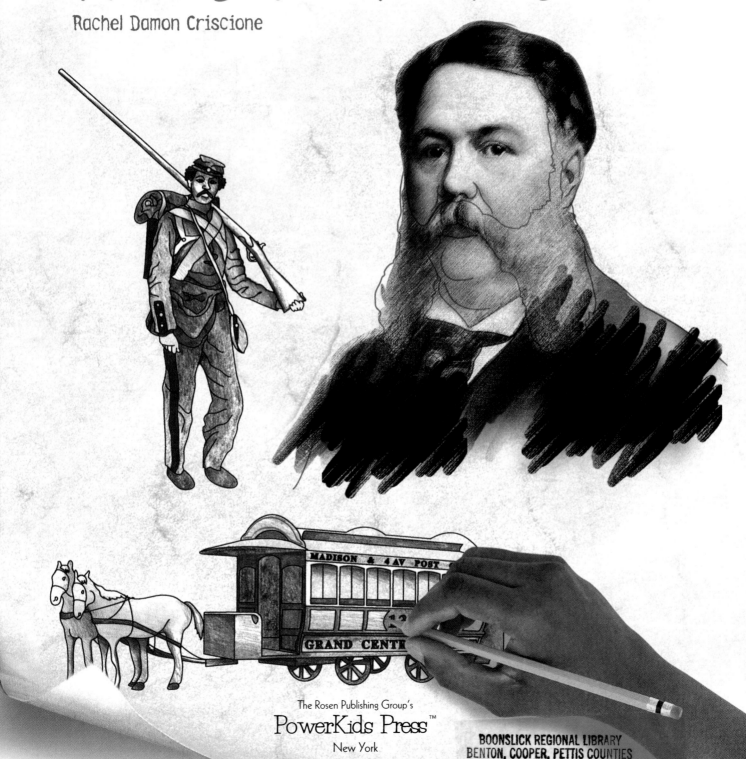

The Rosen Publishing Group's
PowerKids Press™
New York

To Clifton and Anita Damon, my parents and my favorite Vermonters

Published in 2006 by The Rosen Publishing Group, Inc.
29 East 21st Street, New York, NY 10010

First Edition

Editor: Melissa Acevedo
Layout Design: Elana Davidian

Illustrations: All illustrations by Albert Hanner.
Photo Credits: p. 4 Picture History; pp. 7, 24 © North Wind Picture Archives; pp. 8, 9 Vermont Division for Historic Preservation; p. 10 Union College; pp. 12, 18, 26, 28 © Bettman/Corbis; p. 14 © Corbis; p. 16 © Getty Images; p. 20 Library of Congress Prints and Photographs Division; p. 22 (left) National Archives; p. 22 (right) Library of Congress (801). .

Library of Congress Cataloging-in-Publication Data

Criscione, Rachel Damon.
How to draw the life and times of Chester A. Arthur / Rachel Criscione.
p. cm. — (A kid's guide to drawing the presidents of the United States of America) Includes bibliographical references and index. ISBN 1-4042-2998-1
1. Arthur, Chester Alan, 1829–1886—Juvenile literature. 2. Presidents—United States—Biography—Juvenile literature. 3. Drawing—Technique—Juvenile literature. I. Title. II. Series.

E692.C75 2006
743.4'3—dc22
2004025408

Manufactured in the United States of America

Contents

From the Green Mountains to the White House

Chester Alan Arthur, the twenty-first president of the United States, was born on October 5, 1829, in Fairfield, Vermont, in a simple log cabin. He was the oldest boy in a family of two boys and five girls. His father, William Arthur, was a Baptist minister who often found work

preaching at different churches. This meant that the family had to move from town to town in both New York and Vermont. Arthur was taught to read and to write at home by his father. In 1839, when they moved to Union Village, New York, Arthur attended school for the first time at the local high school.

In 1845, when Arthur was 15 years old, he entered Union College in Schenectady, New York. Arthur was an excellent student, and it only took him three years to graduate from college. After graduating in 1848, Arthur taught school and studied law until he had saved enough money to move to New York City. When Arthur moved to New York City in 1853, he worked as a law clerk in the office of E. D. Culver. After becoming a lawyer in 1854, Arthur became involved with the Republican political party. Through his party connections, he held various government jobs, including quartermaster general of the New York State military in 1862. This job was important because Arthur was put in charge of all of New York State's military supplies. Being quartermaster general enabled him to slowly become a powerful figure in the Republican Party. In 1880, he was elected vice president of the United States. He later became president in 1881, when President James A. Garfield was assassinated.

You will need the following supplies to draw the life and times of Chester A. Arthur:

✓ A sketch pad   ✓ An eraser   ✓ A pencil   ✓ A ruler

These are some of the shapes and drawing terms you need to know:

Horizontal Line	——	Squiggly Line	⌇
Oval	⬭	Trapezoid	⏢
Rectangle	▭	Triangle	△
Shading	▬	Vertical Line	|
Slanted Line	/	Wavy Line	∿

The Presidential Oath of Office

After the death of President Garfield, Chester Arthur took the presidential oath of office on the morning of September 20, 1881. During his presidency, Arthur made many important changes. He was responsible for increasing the size of the navy. He also asked Congress to fund boats for the navy made only from steel. In doing so Arthur took the first step toward making the United States a leading naval power.

Arthur also fought for changes in the civil service system. The system had become dishonest because government jobs were given only to people who were faithful political party members. In 1883, the Pendleton Civil Service Act was passed. This law required people seeking federal jobs to pass a test before they were hired to work for the U.S. government. When his presidential term ended in 1884, Arthur did not actively seek a second term because his health was poor. By not being elected to a second term, Arthur remains one of the few U.S. presidents who was never elected to office.

Chester Arthur was sworn in as president of the United States of America the morning after James Garfield died. This hand-colored woodcut shows Arthur taking the oath of office at his home in New York City on September 20, 1881.

Chester Arthur's Vermont

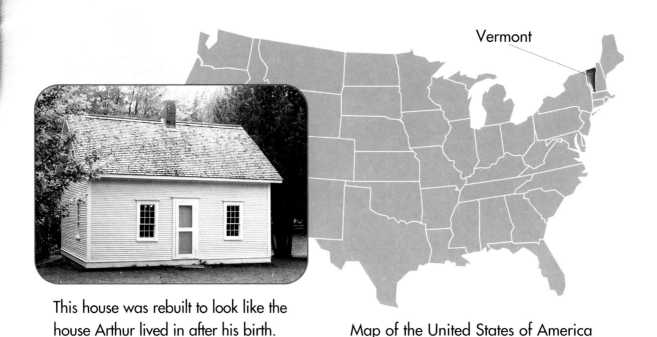

This house was rebuilt to look like the house Arthur lived in after his birth.

Map of the United States of America

Fairfield, the small town in Vermont where Chester Arthur was born in 1829, is nestled between Lake Champlain and the Canadian border. In the 1800s, Fairfield was not a rich town. The members of the Baptist church had to struggle to build a house for their new preacher, William Arthur, and his family. While their house was being built, the Arthur family lived in a log cabin near the church. It was in this cabin that Arthur was born. Today a monument marks the place where the cabin once stood. It was torn down years ago. In 1953, the state of Vermont, using old pictures of the house, built a house similar to the one Arthur's family lived in after he was born. The house was built on land near the monument.

The North Fairfield Baptist Church is located a short distance away from Arthur's home. The building that stands there today is a reconstruction of the church where Arthur's father used to preach. The church, which still has no electricity, was given to the state of Vermont in 1970. Today both the church and the Arthur home are open to the public from the late spring through the fall.

This old brick church was constructed to look like the building in which Arthur's father used to preach.

School Days at Union College

In 1839, the Arthur family left their home in Fairfield, Vermont, to move to Union Village, modern-day Greenwich, New York. While in Union Village, Chester Arthur attended Lyceum, a local school that prepared boys for college. In 1845, when he was 15 years old,  he entered Union College in Schenectady, New York, to study liberal arts. Union College's seal is shown above. During his school vacations, Arthur worked as a teacher to help pay his room and board costs of $125 per year and his college tuition of $28.

In the late 1840s, Union College had many students whose fathers were involved in politics. Arthur made many friends at Union College who would help him later on with his political career. After he graduated in 1848, Arthur continued to teach school, and he studied law on his own. In 1852, he became the principal of a school in Cohoes, New York. He worked there until he had saved up money to move to New York City.

1 The woman that appears on the Union College seal is Minerva, Roman goddess of knowledge. The seal was first created in 1795. To draw the seal, start with a large oval. Add a smaller oval inside the larger one. Add another oval inside the smaller one as shown.

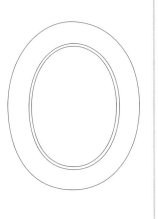

2 Inside the smallest oval, draw an oval. This will be a guide for the face of Minerva. Draw a circle that connects to the oval as shown. Draw curved shapes on the top and bottom of the drawing to make banners.

3 Using the oval face guide, draw the shape of Minerva's face and neck as shown. The bottom of her neck ends in a point. Use the circle guide to draw her hat. Use lines to create her hair. Add detail between the two ovals from step 1 as shown.

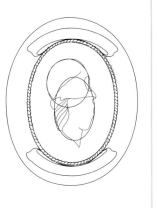

4 Erase all extra lines. Draw the shapes on both the left and right sides of the ovals from step 1. There should be five shapes on either side. Add the shapes on the top and bottom of the curved shapes from step 2. There should be five shapes on top and five on the bottom.

5 Add the words "ST: OF N: YORK" to the top curved shape. Add "UNION COLLEGE 1795" to the bottom shape. Add Minerva's eyes, ear, eyebrows, nose, and mouth. Add a line below her mouth for the chin. Add lines to her hair. Add the words and star that appear in the seal.

6 To finish Union College's seal, shade in the words you added in step 5. Add light shading to the seal as shown. Excellent work!

11

Arthur Becomes a Lawyer

Chester Arthur continued to study law when he moved to New York City in 1853. He became a lawyer in 1854, and started working in the law

office of E. D. Culver, where he helped with the *Lemmon* slave case. The case involved a Virginian man who brought his eight African American slaves with him to visit New York. In 1860, the court ruled that all slaves were free while they were visiting New York State.

Arthur was also a part of the *Elizabeth Jennings* case in 1855. Jennings was an African American teacher in New York City who sat in the "white people only" section of a city streetcar, like the one shown above. The driver forced her off the streetcar, and the case was brought to court. Arthur argued for her in court, and Jennings won the case. The court ruled that everyone in New York City, regardless of the color of their skin, could sit anywhere they wanted to on city streetcars.

1

Streetcars in this time period were led by horses. The picture of this New York City streetcar was taken in 1884. Draw a large rectangle to start.

2

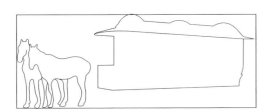

Inside the rectangle draw the two shapes of the horses as shown. Then draw the shape of the streetcar as shown.

3

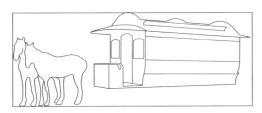

Add a thin shape and a curved line to the roof. Add lines to the right side. Add lines to the front of the streetcar. Add two windows and a door.

4

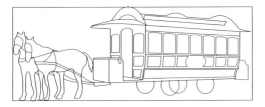

Add curved lines to the roof as shown. Add shapes along the right side of the streetcar for windows and detail. Add shapes near the door as shown. Add a shape to the back of the streetcar. Draw four half circles as shown for wheels. Add reins and harnesses to the horses. Add a tail.

5

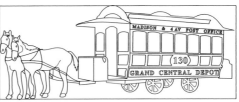

Add the horses' eyes, manes, noses, and hooves. Add lines to their bodies for detail. Add another tail. Add a shape close to the front wheels of the streetcar. Add spokes to the wheels. Add the words and number that appear on the side of the streetcar.

6

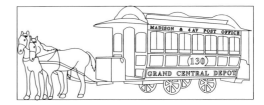

Add both horizontal and vertical lines to the windows on the right side. Add lines and shapes to the back of the streetcar as shown.

7

To finish your streetcar, shade in the picture. Some parts of the streetcar are darker than others. Beautiful work!

Ellen Lewis Herndon Arthur

Ellen Lewis Herndon was born on August 30, 1837, in Culpeper, Virginia. She was the only child of William Lewis Herndon, a famous officer in the navy, and his wife Elizabeth. As a young girl, Ellen had a beautiful singing voice. She drew much attention when she sang with  the choir at St. John's Episcopal Church on Lafayette Square, in Washington, D.C. Ellen first met Chester Arthur in 1856 in New York City. Ellen instantly liked Arthur in spite of their different backgrounds. They were married on October 25, 1859. Ellen and Arthur had three children and a very happy marriage. They both shared an interest in the latest styles of clothing and in fancy dinner parties.

Ellen died of pneumonia, an illness of the lungs, while in New York in January 1880. Her husband became president a year and a half later. During his time in the White House, Arthur had fresh flowers placed next to a picture of Ellen every day.

1

The picture on page 14 of Ellen Lewis Herndon Arthur was taken sometime during the nineteenth century. To begin draw a large rectangle.

2

Draw an oval. This will be the guide for her head. Draw a curved line that comes out from the bottom of the oval for her neck. Draw the guides for her body.

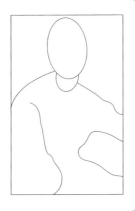

3

Add an oval on the right side as a guide for her hand. Add two lines and three circles to the head guide. These will be the guides for her eyes, nose, and mouth.

4

Using squiggly lines, draw in Ellen's clothes, including her collar, sleeves, and waistline. Add two curved shapes to the right for her chair. Using the oval head guide, add her hair. Draw her ear and earring. Add her chin, cheek, eyebrows, eyes, nose, and mouth.

5

Erase all the head, face, and body guides. Add straight and squiggly lines to Ellen's clothing. These lines show the folds in the cloth.

6

Add curved and wavy lines to her hair. Add two short curved lines underneath her eyes. Draw her hand in the oval guide. Draw the ring that is on her finger. Add four circles for buttons, and the shape above them.

7

Erase the oval hand guide and the rectangular guide from step 1. Finish your drawing of Ellen Lewis Herndon Arthur with shading. Her hair and clothes are darker than her hand and face. Great job!

The Quartermaster General and the Union Army

By 1861, Chester Arthur had become heavily involved in the Republican Party. The Republican governor of New York rewarded Arthur for his support by appointing him assistant quartermaster general of New York. The job included clothing, feeding, and providing shelter for more than 220,000 volunteers in the New York State military. Soon after the Civil War began, Arthur was made quartermaster general. He was now responsible for all the Union soldiers who passed through New York on their way to fight in the South. Arthur had to make sure that the soldiers had all the clothing and supplies they needed, as the Union soldier above has. Arthur was good at his job and was highly respected by those who worked for him. He was replaced as quartermaster general in 1863, two years before the Union won the war. Arthur lost his position because Republicans were no longer in power in New York.

1 This picture of a Union soldier in uniform was taken around 1861. To draw him start with a rectangle. Inside the rectangle draw the guide for the body using ovals. Next draw the shape for the gun.

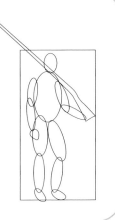

2 Add the soldier's eyes, eyebrows, moustache, nose, and mouth. Add a hat on his head, an ear, and hair coming out from the sides. Add a hand holding the end of the gun. Add lines for clothing.

3 Begin drawing the soldier's backpack. Add clothing lines to the lower part of the Union soldier's body. Draw his left hand using the oval guide.

4 Erase extra lines. Add the shapes on the soldier's chest. Add the shoulder strap and the pack that hangs on his side. Add lines and shapes on his clothing. Add buttons and detail to his sleeve.

5 Add more lines across the soldier's chest. Add a long stripe down the side of one pant leg. Add more lines to his clothing for detail.

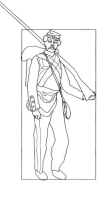

6 Add a line for the soldier's left ear. Add small circles inside his eyes. Add short, rough lines across his legs, chest, and arms to create folds in his clothing. Add detail to the backpack.

7 Erase the rectangle guide from step 1. Add shapes and lines to the bottom of the gun for detail.

8 Finish your drawing of the Union soldier by shading. Notice which parts of the drawing are darker. What a great drawing!

Political Party Life

Despite being saddened over losing the quartermaster general position, Chester Arthur continued to be an active member of the Republican Party. This brought him to the attention of Roscoe Conkling, a Republican Party leader in New York. Conkling and Arthur formed a new political party, called the Stalwart Republicans. The Stalwart Party operated on the spoils system, in which faithful party members were rewarded with government jobs. In return they had to contribute time and money to the party. Through the spoils system, Arthur was appointed collector of customs for the Port of New York. With more than 1,000 workers, the port was the largest federal office in the country. At the time Arthur was a firm believer in the spoils system, and he hired people if they were good Stalwarts. When Rutherford Hayes became president, he fired Arthur in 1878. He thought that Arthur's hiring practices were unfair. Arthur returned to his law practice in New York. The Republican Party symbol is shown above.

1

The elephant is the symbol of the Republican Party. Created by Thomas Nast, the Republican elephant was first shown to the public in 1874. To start draw a large rectangle.

2

Draw a large circle in the rectangle. Draw the circle so that it is in the upper right corner. It touches the top and right side of the rectangle.

3

Draw a smaller circle that connects with the larger one. This smaller circle will be the guide for the elephant's head.

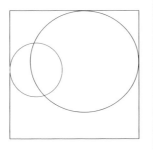

4

Using the head guide from step 3, draw the elephant's head, ear, trunk, tusks, and mouth. Draw a circle for the elephant's eye. Add a smaller circle inside the eye.

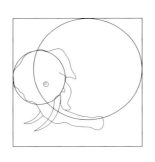

5

Using the large circle guide from step 2, draw in the body of the elephant. Add four legs. Add lines to the ear and mouth.

6

Add lines to the face and body of the elephant for detail. Add a shape to the end of the trunk for an opening. Add lines to the feet for toes.

7

Erase the head and body guides. Erase the rectangle, too. Add the words "THE REPUBLICAN VOTE" to the body.

8

Finish your drawing of the Republican elephant by shading. Good work!

Vice President Arthur

After losing his position as collector of customs, Chester Arthur helped make the Stalwarts a powerful party while practicing law in New York. He returned to public office when he was nominated as James Garfield's running mate in the 1880 presidential election. The poster above is from their campaign. Many voters did not trust Arthur because of his relationship with Roscoe Conkling. They feared that if Arthur became vice president, Conkling would be running the country. Voters wanted to vote for Garfield without having to vote for Arthur. In 1880, Garfield and Arthur won the election by a small number of votes. They took office in March 1881. A short time later, on July 2, 1881, President Garfield was shot at a train station in Washington, D.C., by an angry man who had not gotten the government job he had wanted. When Garfield died Arthur was sworn in as president on September 20, 1881. Arthur became the third U.S. president in a six-month period.

1

This 1880 campaign poster was published by Haasis & Lubrecht. Lady Peace appears between the pictures of James Garfield and Chester Arthur. To draw Lady Peace, start with a long rectangle.

2

Draw one circle, three ovals, and a curved line. These shapes should all overlap with one another. They will be the guide for the head and body of Lady Peace.

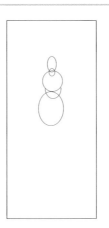

3

Draw a rectangular shape that comes from the bottom oval. Add curved lines and three circles coming out of the rectangular shape. Add Lady Peace's hair and guides for her arms.

4

Use the arm guides to draw the arms and hands. Then use the body guide to outline the body. Draw the cloth around her waist. Draw the shapes at the bottom of her gown and in the lower middle circle.

5

Erase extra lines. Add vertical lines to Lady Peace's gown for the folds. Add the shapes and lines behind Lady Peace as shown. These will be the guides for the flags.

6

Add lines to the flags' bottoms to make it appear as if they are striped. Add lines to the tops of the flags. Draw Lady Peace's nose, mouth, eyes, and eyebrows. Add a line to her waist.

7

Add shapes to Lady Peace's stand. Add lines to the bottom of her gown for folds.

8

Finish your drawing of Lady Peace with shading. Some parts of the drawing are darker than others. Keep this in mind when shading. Excellent work!

The Gentleman Boss

Even though most people in the United States were unhappy about it, Chester Arthur was president. He refused to move his family into the White House until it was remodeled. He had 24 wagonloads of furniture taken away from the White House and sold at an auction. He hired Louis Tiffany, a famous New York designer, to redecorate the White House. Tiffany put in a famous Tiffany screen and floor tiles in the entrance hall of the White House, as shown above in the photo and drawing. Arthur also had the White House's first elevator and indoor plumbing put in. Congress funded this project, which cost more than $30,000. When the remodeling was completed late in 1881, Arthur, his sister, and his daughter moved into the White House.

Arthur was known as a man of fine taste. All his suits were made of the best cloth. Soon people started to call Chester Arthur the Gentleman Boss, in honor of his expensive taste and good manners.

1

When Louis Tiffany remodeled the White House, he added beautiful tiles to the entrance hall. To draw one of the tiles, start with a square. Add a shape with eight points inside the square.

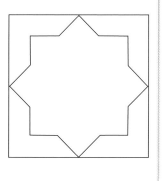

2

Inside the eight-pointed shape, draw two smaller eight-pointed shapes. Then add a square inside the smallest shape. Draw a small circle in the center.

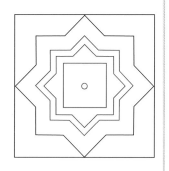

3

Inside the inner square, draw three circles. Draw another circle around the circle from step 2. Add four circles surrounding that circle as shown.

4

Add diamond shapes to four points of the second eight-pointed shape. Add a square with a circle inside it to each remaining point. Add lines to connect the shapes as shown. Erase extra lines.

5

Add two squares around the circles in the middle of the tile as shown. Add four small triangles around it as shown. Add small circles in the diamonds and circles from step 4.

6

Add small squares and lines inside the lines that connect the shapes from step 4.

7

Erase the large square guide box. Add a smaller, upside-down triangle inside each of the triangles from step 5. Add shapes and detail lines to the center as shown.

8

To complete the drawing of the tile from the entrance hall of the White House, shade it in with your pencil. Pat yourself on the back! You did a great job!

The Star Route Fraud

In 1881, many people feared that Chester Arthur was unfit to be president because of his ties with Roscoe Conkling and the spoils system. They felt that Arthur would do what was best for his friends, not what was best for the country. He ended up proving them wrong during the Star Route Fraud.

Star Routes were mail routes the U.S. Post Office could not get to because they were in rustic areas. The government paid private companies to bring mail to these routes. When Garfield was still in office, two men were put on trial for accepting federal money for mail routes that did not exist. People thought Arthur would end the trial when he became president. Instead he ordered that the trial continue. This caused a split between Arthur and the Stalwarts. The illegal activities stopped, and many people considered Arthur to be the one who put an end to the mail fraud. The cartoon above is based on the Star Route Fraud.

1

In 1881, Thomas Nast drew this cartoon of the postmaster in the Star Route Fraud. To draw the mailbag with the stars and scorpion falling out, start with a long rectangle.

2

Draw the shape of the bag in the upper right corner of the rectangle. Add a curved line to the top of the bag.

3

Draw four circles. They should look like they are falling out of the bag. The circle closest to the bottom is the largest. The other three circles are smaller.

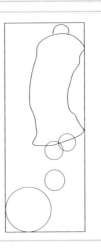

4

Add lines to the top of the bag to create a handle. Add a rough line to the left side and bottom of the bag. Use curved lines to make the bag's opening. Add circles and ovals to the side and bottom.

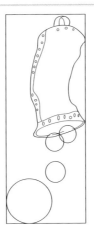

5

Inside the three smaller circles you drew in step 3, add stars. Add half of another star as if it is just about to fall out of the bag.

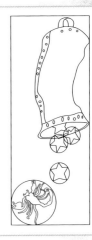

6

Draw the scorpion as shown in the largest circle at the bottom of the rectangle. A scorpion is a type of insect that has a poisonous stinger.

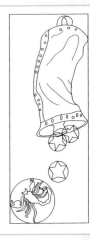

7

Add lines to the bag as shown. These lines are to show folds in the bag.

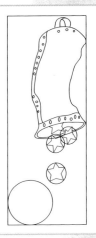

8

Erase all the guides and any extra lines. Add a line coming out from the right side of the bag. Finish your drawing by shading. The scorpion in this picture stands for fraud. Great work!

The Pendleton Civil Service Act

Before Chester Arthur became president, he was a supporter of the spoils system. However, once in office, Arthur turned against

POST-OFFICE, WASHINGTON.

the spoils system and many of the people who helped put him into power. He became a supporter of government change.

In 1883, Arthur signed the Pendleton Civil Service Act. The act changed the way the government hired workers for federal offices, like the U.S. Post Office, shown above. Government jobs were no longer handed out as rewards to political party members. People had to pass a test that showed they had the skills needed to do the job. Once a person was hired, the Pendleton Act made it illegal to fire anyone for political reasons. People no longer had to give money to political parties to keep their jobs. The Pendleton Act made Arthur's fellow Stalwarts angry, especially his old friend Roscoe Conkling. The Pendleton Act was the start of today's U.S. civil service system.

1

To draw the U.S. Post Office in Washington, D.C., start with a rectangle.

2

Inside the rectangular guide, draw the front and side of the building using a rectangle and a square. Add lines across the bottom of the drawing as shown.

3

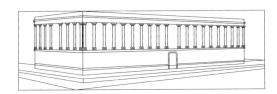

Add a door to the middle of the bottom of the building. Add lines across the base of the building. Draw vertical columns on both sides of the building.

4

In the space between the columns, add windows. The bottom windows have tiny triangles on top of them. Be sure to add them to your drawing.

5

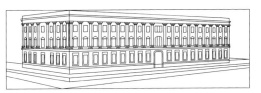

Add the windows along the bottom of the post office building.

6

Add horizontal and vertical lines to the top of the building. Add two pointed shapes to the roof. Add vertical lines across the bottom of the building. This will be the start of the fence. Add steps in front of the door.

7

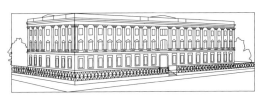

Finish drawing the fence around the building by adding diamond shapes as shown. Draw a tree on either side of the post office.

8

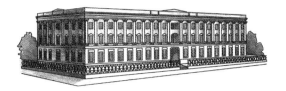

Erase the rectangular guide from step 1. Finish your drawing by shading in the building. Good job!

The Death of Chester A. Arthur

Chester A. Arthur learned early in his presidential term that he had a kidney disease called Bright's disease. He decided to keep his disease a secret because he knew there was no cure and his health was beginning to fail. He realized that he would not live out a second term. After the Republican Party chose another man as their presidential candidate in 1884, Arthur returned to his law practice in New York City. He was a private man, so he burned his personal papers shortly before he died. Arthur died at home on November 18, 1886. He was buried at Albany Rural Cemetery in Albany, New York.

Arthur proved to be an honorable president who put the needs of the American people before everything else. He always did what he thought was the right thing, even if it cost him many friends. Arthur's honesty and commitment to the American people let him lead the United States into a new age.

1

Ole Peter Hansen Balling painted this undated picture of President Chester Arthur. To start draw a rectangle.

2

Inside the rectangle add a large oval. Then use curved lines to draw the shape that will become his shoulders and body.

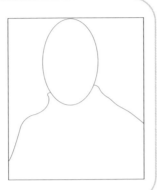

3

Draw in Arthur's collar using straight and curved lines. Add a circle for a button on the left side.

4

Inside the oval draw a smaller oval. It should line up with the large oval on the left side. Draw a curved horizontal line and a vertical line that cross in the middle. Draw three circles and a line for his eyes, nose, and mouth. Add his ear.

5

Using rough lines and shapes, draw in his hair as shown. Then add his eyebrows above the circle guides for his eyes.

6

Add lines and circles in his eyes. Use the circular guide to draw his nose. Draw his beard. Add a line for his chin and his neck.

7

Add another line to Arthur's mouth. Add lines around his eyes as shown.

8

Erase the guides and any extra lines. Finish your drawing by shading. You are all done! Great job!

Timeline

1829 Chester Alan Arthur is born in Fairfield, Vermont, on October 5.

1845 At the age of 15, Arthur enters Union College in Schenectady, New York.

1848 Arthur graduates from Union College.

1853 Arthur moves to New York City to study law.

1854 Chester Arthur becomes a lawyer in New York City.

1855 Arthur argues for Elizabeth Jennings in court and wins the case.

1859 Arthur marries Ellen Herndon Lewis on October 25.

1862 Arthur is named quartermaster general of New York State.

1871 Arthur is appointed by President Ulysses S. Grant to be the collector of customs for the Port of New York.

1880 Ellen Arthur dies of pneumonia.

Chester Arthur is elected vice president of the United States.

1881 President Garfield is killed.

Chester Arthur becomes the twenty-first president of the United States.

1882 Arthur finds out he has Bright's disease.

1883 President Arthur signs the Pendleton Civil Service Act into law.

1884 Arthur's presidential term ends. The Republican Party does not nominate him for the upcoming election.

1886 Arthur dies on November 18 and is buried in Albany, New York.

Glossary

assassinated (uh-SA-suh-nayt-ed) Killed suddenly, often by secret attack.

auction (OK-shun) A sale at which goods are sold to whoever pays the most.

campaign (kam-PAYN) A plan to get a certain result, such as to win an election.

choir (KWY-er) A group of people who sing together.

civil service (SIH-vul SER-vis) Having to do with government jobs that are now appointed through the aid of tests.

Civil War (SIH-vul WOR) The war fought between the Northern and the Southern states of America from 1861 to 1865.

customs (KUS-tumz) The taxes on goods entering or leaving the country.

designer (dih-ZY-nur) A person who creates plans for a new product.

disease (dih-ZEEZ) An illness or sickness.

fraud (FROD) The use of lies or tricks to cheat or to take advantage of a situation in a way that is against the law.

involved (in-VOLVD) Kept busy by something.

liberal arts (LIB-rul ARTS) Studies in college that usually consist of subjects like English, history, and languages.

nestled (NEH-suld) Curled up next to.

nominated (NAH-muh-nayt-ed) Suggested that someone or something should be given an award or a position.

oath (OHTH) A promise.

plumbing (PLUH-ming) Pipes that carry water to and from a building.

political party (puh-LIH-tih-kul PAR-tee) A group of people who have similar beliefs in how the government affairs should be run.

symbol (SIM-bul) An object or a picture that stands for something else.

tuition (tuh-WIH-shun) Money paid to receive instruction at a school.

volunteers (vah-lun-TEERZ) Soldiers who had jobs outside the military before the war.

Index

Web Sites

Due to the changing nature of Internet links, PowerKids Press has developed an online list of Web sites related to the subject of this book. This site is updated regularly. Please use this link to access the list:
www.powerkidslinks.com/kgdpusa/carthur/